101 SCRIPTURE VERSES & MEDITATIONS

SELECT BIBLE PASSAGES FOR
INSPIRATION, AFFIRMATION, & DECLARATION,
WITH TIPS FOR MEMORIZATION

ANN MARIE RANDALL

CONTENTS

All Scripture passages taken from the
Revised Standard Version (RSV)

1

INTRODUCTION

The Bible is daunting for most of us. This book breaks down the mountain of Scripture that is the Bible. I have selected beautiful and powerful passages that speak to the heart and inspire. Because these passages bring life to the heart, they will be easier to memorize if you so desire. In addition, meditations and commentaries are provided. There are several ways to help with scripture coming alive in your heart and life. These tools are: inspiration, declaration, proclamation, and agreement.

Inspiration: This simply means that you awaken your spiritual senses and "hear" what God is saying to you. In your body you have 5 senses, your soul has 5 parallel senses: spiritual sight, spiritual hearing, spiritual taste, spiritual smelling, and spiritual touch. Many times, one of these senses is the normative way that God touches your soul. Do you know your preferred sense? The one that God uses most often to communicate to you a sensate presence of Himself? You can certainly ask God to expand His sensate presence to you. Before we read scripture, or listen to it, the first thing we should do is ask the Holy

Spirit to be with us and to enliven our spiritual senses. Then, when we read or listen to Scripture, we will be prepared to hear what the Lord would like to say to us. This is where inspiration comes in, as you read or listen to these passages, see what inspires you. Pay attention to where God is tickling your heart!

Listen to God and stay with this sensate experience of God as long as it lasts. This is God speaking into your life today!

Declaration: Declaration is part of speaking the Good News to ourselves. Once we recognize that a passage has inspired us, we declare the truth of that passage to ourselves. This is best accomplished by speaking it out loud to yourself. When we hear our own voice speaking God's words, it is an affirmation that God loves us, that God has spoken to us, and that you declare this to be what you desire in your life: you welcome God's word, God's life, and God's love into your life. Also, when we speak, the thoughts and words come out of ourselves, they come out of our inner being, they come out of our mind, heart, and body. These words go into the world in the form of sound waves. What is spoken out loud can never be taken back. I encourage you to speak God's words, and God's love, and God's life out loud and into your life.

Proclamation: Once you have a passage that has inspired you, and you have proclaimed it to yourself, it is often time to memorize it and share it with the world as the Spirit prompts you. Proclamation is to speak the words of Scripture to another in order to encourage them in their life of faith. As you memorize short passages, and you go throughout your day, the Holy Spirit will point out to you people that He would like you to share this particular scripture with. I encourage you to step out in faith and declare God's holy Word to people, in effect, pouring the love of God into *their* lives!

Agreement: This is perhaps the most powerful method to open your heart to Scripture and the power of Scripture to change your life. When we come into agreement with Scripture, we are telling God "I agree with you" in the specific passage. We are giving God permission to enact the truth of this Scripture in your life right now. Coming into agreement with Scripture also helps to break down walls, barriers, and lies in our life. All of these things prevent us from a deeper relationship with the Lord. When we can break down lies that have been spoken into our life, then the truth of God's love can flood in. This is what we all want. We have all been wounded in one way or another, and God so desires to enter into our life in a deeper way and to heal all of our wounds, wipe away all of our tears.

This book contains beautifully selected powerful passages. Your vulnerability to enter into these passages will be the key to renewing zeal for the Lord in your life.

2

PRAISE

Praise, thanksgiving, and worship are the most efficient ways to get into the presence of God, to enter His throne room and to enjoy heavenly worship while here on earth! Praise has the power to lift us out of the difficulties of daily life and remind us of God's great love for us, and the many graces and blessings that He is pouring out for us and in us every minute of every day. I challenge you to intentionally enter into praise of God throughout each day. This could take a variety of forms, one simple way is to memorize a praise passage and let it be your mantra throughout the day, for a whole day. Another easy way is to praise God for two or three minutes several times sprinkled throughout the day. Praise of the living God will change your life!

I will sing to the Lord all my life,
make music to my God while I live.

- Psalm 104:33

To sing to the Lord all your life and make music to Him means that you are lifting up your entire life and everything that you are to make beautiful music for the Lord. It is trusting Him that He has fearfully and wonderfully made you, and that you can gather up all that you are and lift it up to the Lord and He will delight and rejoice in you. When you feel the warmth of His love, raising your voice to sing and making music to Him is the most natural thing. It's a great joy and delight.

When we feel less than loved or lovable, raising your voice to the Lord can drive out sadness, despair, anxiety, or the doldrums of life. I challenge you in those moments to put on some praise music, and sing *and dance* to the Lord.

Memorization Recommended.

It is good to give thanks to the Lord,
to make music to your name Oh Most High.

- Psalm 92:1

Thanksgiving is another golden nugget. When we give thanks, we need to think about what people and things in our life that we are thankful for. Oftentimes we recognize that things in our life which draw gratitude out of our heart are things that have been given to us, good friends, a good job, a beautiful sunrise, a kind comment from a difficult child. Giving thanks draws us out of our self-centered mindset and encourages us to look at life through the lens of giftedness.

Memorization Recommended.

They are planted in the house of the Lord,

they flourish in the courts of our God.

- Psalm 92:13

To be planted in the House of the Lord means that you are rooted in God. Those who are rooted in God flourish. Don't we all want to flourish? But we have all sinned and fallen short of the glory of God, and so we think we cannot be planted in God's house. This is a lie from a liar and the father of lies. I encourage you to declare this passage to yourself, out loud. I encourage you to come into agreement with this passage and allow the Lord to rain down flourishing in your heart and in your life. When we break the power of lies in our life, then the truth of God can flood in. Dear brothers and sisters in Christ, be planted in the House of the Lord as you declare and come into agreement with God's word in Psalm 92 verse 13.

Memorization Recommended.

Just as the Father raises the dead

and gives life,

so also does the Son give life

to whomever He wishes

- John 5:21

We know the Father raises the dead and gives life, we hear all about that in the Scriptures. The Son also rises from the dead, and He Himself was raised from the dead by the love of the Father. Life and death are not simply physical, there is emotional life and death, psychic life and death, intellectual life and death, emotional life and death. We want life, all life, abundant life, we want the Father and the Son in our corner. Jesus tells us in the Gospel of John that He is the Way, the Truth, and the Life, it is normative and beautiful to go to the Father through the Son. Let us love the Son with our whole heart, and He will give us life, and lead us to our heavenly Father.

Memorization Recommended.

Seek the Lord while he may be found,

call to him while he is near.

- Isaiah 55:6

This is a trick passage! The Lord can always be found, and He is always near. So, it means that we should always be seeking him, and always be calling to him. I love the Lord's humor. Though we may not immediately experience that we have found him, it is much like the sun at night. Do you doubt that the sun is shining on the other side of the world? I do not. The truth is the Lord is always near, so though you may not feel Him at any given moment, declare the truth of this passage and know that He is near, indeed, very near to you!

The Lord is near, call to Him now
and share with Him your day so far.

I formed a people for myself,
that they might announce my praise.

- Isaiah 43:21

Surprise, surprise, we are the people that He formed for Himself! Can you not feel it? Do you not know it? Reject those lies and come into the truth of who you are: a people for our God. That means that we are to announce His praise. It means that we are to be always mindful of the truth of God, all He has done for us, and be willing to give a reason for our hope. When was the last time you worked on your two-minute testimony to share it with a world aching for love? I challenge you to prepare a 2 minute testimony of what God has done for you, so that you might announce His praise as the Holy Spirit prompts you!!

Work on and practice your 2 minute testimony
out loud!!

May my thoughts be pleasing to him.
I find my joy in the Lord!

- Psalm 104:34

We have been talking about praise. There is no doubt that praise is pleasing to God. Are the rest of our thoughts pleasing to Him? Perhaps we need to cleanse some of our thoughts. Perhaps we need to fast from unholy thoughts. Have we wondered how others find joy in the Lord but we do not? Perhaps the key is in this passage, and fasting from the thoughts that are not pleasing to Him. No doubt, to do these things will help us to spontaneously find our joy in the Lord.

Identify 2 thought patterns that are not pleasing to God and commit to fasting from them

How can I repay the Lord's goodness to me?

- Psalm 116:12

For many, this passage falls flat. What is the Lord's goodness to me? Do I owe Him anything? Repayment... That's an interesting question. The real question is, if my experience of the Lord is different from the Scriptures' representation, where is the shortfall? The hard truth is, often, my Christian experience falls dramatically short of what God has promised us in Holy Scripture. The smart thing to do is recognize that I have lowered my expectations. And now I need to raise my eyes to heaven, open my heart, and receive all of the goodness that God is pouring out to me right now. Then I can worry about repayment. First let us experience the abundant goodness that God has for us!

Call upon the Lord, open your heart,
and receive His goodness for you!

Let us come into his presence
with thanksgiving;
let us make a joyful noise to him
with songs of praise!

- Psalm 95:2

This is my kind of passage, when I open my mouth to sing to the Lord, my voice is not melodic, sweet, or harmonious. It is indeed a joyful noise. It may only be joyful to me and it certainly is a noise. The Lord knows it is a joyful noise for Him. On a more serious note, when we give thanksgiving, we come into this presence. Therefore I give thanksgiving often throughout the day so that I know I am in His presence. He hears me, He loves me, and He showers me with blessings!

Declare the truth of this passage and enact it in your life.
Memorization Recommended.

Great is the Lord and greatly to be praised

in the city of our God.

His holy mountain, beautiful in majesty,

is the joy of all the earth.

- Psalm 48:1

In scripture, and in the Old Testament, God's holy mountain is heaven. Let's remember that heaven is a created reality. In the Christian creed we pray "I believe in God the Father almighty, creator of heaven and earth." Thus this passage is inviting us to pray with the heavenly hosts, with all the Saints, with all the angels, and join in heavenly praise. In the Our Father prayer, we ask for God's Kingdom to come, meaning His Kingdom to come down onto the earth where we live right now. Hence, there is only a thin veil between heaven and earth right now, this passage encourages us to pierce through that veil and join in heavenly worship so as to partake of the "joy of all the earth"!

Join in heavenly worship today
however you are inspired to do so!

How lovely is your dwelling place Lord,

God of hosts....

My soul is yearning for the

courts of the Lord.

- Psalm 84:1

What does the dwelling place of the Lord look like? Feel free to peruse Revelation chapter 21. It is indeed a place worthy of yearning for. We are on a pilgrimage right now, this is not our homeland. We need a radical shift in perspective. Our homeland is heaven and this is a sojourn. Indeed I am yearning for the courts of the Lord, and He will sustain me until the day when He welcomes me into my true homeland with Him.

Read Revelation 21 and you will yearn!

O Lord, I love the house where you dwell,

the place where your glory abides.

\- Psalm 26:8

His house and His glory have now become familiar to
me. He lives in my heart as He promised, and His house
and my heart are very near to one another. I indeed love
where He dwells and hope to join Him there. His glory
abides not only in His house but also in His creation.
Look to the sunset, look to the sunrise, look to the power
of the storm and you will see, His glory abides. If we have
eyes to see, His glory is all around us!

Watch a sunrise from the first glimmer of light
to sun full up, and you will see His glory!

Come into his presence with singing!...
Serve the LORD cheerfully.
Come into his presence with joyful songs.

- Psalm 100:2

Again with the singing, what's up with the singing? It must be important. It encourages me to sing, to sing more, and to sing more loudly. My 8th grade teacher told me "If God gave you a good voice, you should give your voice back to Him in joyful song. If He gave you a bad voice, sing even louder because He deserves to hear it!" Aside from singing and singing joyful songs, this passage teaches us to serve the Lord cheerfully. It means that serving the Lord *is a cheerful thing*, if we are struggling to serve Him in this way, we should entreat the Lord to pour out this grace, He surely desires to pour out cheerfulness.

In the morning, ask the Lord for cheerfulness.
Monitor your heart throughout the day
for the outpouring of this grace.

Enter his gates with thanksgiving,

and his courts with praise!

Give thanks to him and bless his name.

- Psalm 100:4

Thanksgiving indeed is the key to entering His heavenly court, being with Him, and joining with all those who love the Lord. If our prayer is dull, and our life is a bit drab, thanksgiving is always an excellent activity. Thanksgiving ushers us into His court, into His presence, into His heart.

Spend 10 minutes thanking and praising the Lord
out loud for all the blessings in your life
(the car is a great place to do this).

Where shall we find strength to praise him?
For he is greater than all his works.
Terrible is the Lord and very great,
marvelous is his power.
When you praise the Lord,
exalt him as much as you can;
For he will surpass even that.
When you exalt him,
put forth all of your strength,
and do not grow weary,
for you cannot praise him enough.

- Sirach 43:28-30

Here we wrestle with the strength to praise. Did any of us realize that praise took strength? It is another place in Scripture and in our relationship with the Lord where everything is turned upside down. I think of strength in terms of working out, or lifting weights, or strength to raise a rebellious teenager. But do I really need strength to praise God? Apparently I do, and so do you. To gain strength in different areas of our life, it takes practice, it takes working out, it takes perseverance. I believe the same is true for praise of God. Praising God takes practice, work, and perseverance. So, begin today and raise a glad cry to the Lord!

Praise God today for 5 continuous minutes.

But I, through the greatness of your love,

have access to your house,

I will worship in your holy temple

in fear of thee.

- Psalm 5:7

It is only by God's love that we have access to His house. He has given us a key to His mansion, and invited us to come. His house is the home of my heart and vice versa. To worship God in holy fear is simply to recognize the immensity, infinity, and power of the one true God. Fear of God is the knowledge that my heart and mind can never contain Him, only by His grace does He live in my heart and even then, I am filled with holy fear and trembling.

Meditate on the fact that God's love
is what gives us access to His mansion!
He has given you a key, come on in!
Memorization Recommended.

Praise the Lord!

Praise God in his sanctuary,

praise him in his mighty firmament!

Praise him for his mighty deeds,

Praise him according to his

exceeding greatness!

- Psalm 150:1-2

We are invited here to join God in His sanctuary in heaven. In order to do so, we are directed to collect the mighty deeds that He has done in our own life. This might take some time and some thought. At this moment in history, we are fixated on the self-made man, and often do not think of God and His actions in our lives. The passage above challenges this current framework. Take the time to identify two of Gods' mighty deeds in your life and then join with the Angels and the Saints to praise Him for His greatness!

Memorization Recommended.

Behold, the dwelling place of God

is with the human race.

- Revelation 21:3

This is pure joy. In God's holy word He is proclaiming and promising that His dwelling, the place of His home, the place He desires to be, the place that He is, is with us! God is with us as a race, He is with us individually. This is one of the claims of Christianity that is literally unbelievable, it is simply too good to be true. I encourage you to stretch and to receive God's grace to expand your heart and your mind to believe this beautiful passage. And to enjoy God dwelling with you, personally, in intimate friendship.

Memorization Recommended.

3

SIN, MERCY & FORGIVENESS

For all have sinned and fallen short
of the glory of God.

- Romans 3:23

Sin is a difficult topic. One that most of us shy away
from. Ironically, knowing our sins is what actually
draws us close to God! In the first chapter of Luke, verse
77 it states that "we gain knowledge of salvation by the
forgiveness of our sins." Jesus came to save us and set
us free. What do you suppose He came to save us from?
What kind of slavery do you think we were in that we
needed to be set free? Sin, sin, and more sin. Thus, if we
ignore our sin, salvation is lost to us. God is not afraid
of sin. He has the remedy. Think of a small child making
a mistake, being rambunctious in the living room and
tipping over a plant with soil spilled all over the carpet.
The child runs and hides. You discover it in the next
hour. Are you angry with the child? Of course not! It is
a teaching moment, and you take advantage of it. The
time spent by the child of running and hiding prior to
your discovery is agony for the child. If they had come

to you right away they could have spared themselves all that agony. This is the dynamic of sin. The sooner we go running to our Father in heaven, the sooner we can be forgiven and clean up the mess with Him. The longer we wait before going to God with our sin, the more twisted our insides become. Jesus said that when He was lifted up from the earth, He would draw all things to Himself. Let your sin be drawn into the heart of Jesus, He has already paid the price for sin on the Cross, so why would you ever hold onto your sin? Do you think you have unique sin that God has never heard of before? Do you have a new sin that thousands of years of human beings have never committed before? Ha, reject that lie and go to your Father in heaven and He will forgive you, embrace you, and pour His infinite mercy into your life.

We have sinned,

been wicked,

done evil,

rebelled,

departed from your law.

- Daniel 9:5

We must acknowledge our wrongdoing. Both Daniel and Paul tell us that we have all sinned and fallen short of the glory of God. But we have a Savior who is rich in compassion and forgiveness. In the presence of God there is No Fear in presenting our sins to Him. He is all love and all forgiveness. If you are feeling shame, guilt, anxiety, fear, despair, or the like with regard to your sins this is from your enemy, and the enemy of the human race. The enemy wants to keep you in your sin and keep you away from the merciful compassion and love of God. Reject his silly tactics, place yourself in the presence of our all loving and all merciful God. Proclaim the truth of this passage, break the lies of sin, and be free.

Read this passage aloud, come into formal agreement with it, name your sins and receive forgiveness and peace!

May the Lord, who is good,

grant pardon to all those resolved to seek God,

the Lord, the God of our fathers,

though they be not clean as holiness requires.

\- 2 Chronicles 30:18-19

The key in this passage is resolution to seek the Lord. If our hearts, eyes, and mind are fixed on Jesus, we are resolved. Again we see that holiness requires cleanliness of life, this means bringing all of our shortcomings to the Lord. The reward here is pardon. It is a promise, it is the word of God which is always trustworthy and true. Be resolved and you will be granted pardon today!

Express your resolution to God, give your life to God today, proclaim Jesus to be your Lord and Savior today!!

With age-old love I have loved you,

so I have kept my mercy towards you.

- Jeremiah 31:3

Age-old love, this is speaking towards God's creative power in making you, knitting you together in your mother's womb. He loved you before the dawn of creation, He knew you in His heart before the first star was made. He longs for fellowship with you and towards that end, He has removed the obstacle of sin by the victory of the Cross. He has indeed kept His mercy towards each one of us. I encourage you to believe in His mercy, trust in His mercy, and receive it generously because He pours it out generously.

Declare the truth of this passage and come into formal agreement with it. Renounce unbelief by saying, "In the name of Jesus, I renounce the spirit of unbelief, I come into agreement with this passage and receive God's love and mercy."

Memorization Recommended.

Who can stand when he appears?

- Malachi 3:2

We can only read this passage and understand what it means when we understand the immensity of God, the goodness of God, and the glory of God. He is all good and we are sinful creatures: weak, proud, self-centered. We can stand when He appears only because of our brother Jesus. By Baptism we are adopted into the family of God. By this adoption, we become brothers and sisters of Jesus, the King of Kings and the Lord of Lords. When Jesus walked the earth, He taught us the Our Father prayer. In that first word of that prayer the truth of our adoption is proclaimed. He is truly our brother and we are washed clean by His blood. He stands beside us before the Father, His Father and our Father!

Memorize this passage and proclaim that you can stand when He appears because of your brother Jesus Christ!

We have all sinned and fallen short of the glory of God.

- Romans 3:23

This passage is incredibly freeing. It simply proclaims the truth that each one of us knows to be true in our own heart: the darkness, wickedness, and deception that is present there. It is only freeing if we read it, believe it, and accept it in the presence of God and His overflowing mercy and forgiveness. If we read this passage and pray this passage outside of the context of God's love, we fall into despair, deep despair. Dear brothers and sisters, never leave the presence of God, and we can receive the truth of this passage knowing that mercy is ours for the asking, again and again as we grow in grace and move away from sin towards the glory of God.

Memorization Recommended.

A bruised reed he will not break,

a smoldering wick he will not quench.

- Isaiah 42:3

Imagine yourself as this reed or as this wick, it is small and insignificant, it is broken and without hope. This is you, and this is me. Notice the gentleness, notice the tenderness of the God here. Our Lord, the King of Kings will not break us and will not snuff us out. This is a promise. The Lord loves when we speak to Him in His own words. When you are low and without hope, when you are alone and feel unloved, when you are that reed or that wick, call out to the Lord in these words and claim the promise that you will not be broken, you will not be snuffed out. Call upon the Lord's love and mercy, open your heart and let Him pour it in.

Memorization Recommended.

O Lord, hold not back,

for you are our Father.

- Isaiah 63:16

No matter what your own father was like, the truth of God the Father is that He is all loving, all knowing, and all good. Here, in this passage, we ask our Father in heaven to not hold back, that means to give more, and more, and more. Our God is a God of always more: more love, more mercy, more peace, more joy. It is difficult for us to understand this because of our limited nature. We are small, we are finite, but He is infinite. Grace is the power of God to expand our heart and our mind to receive the infinity of God. Beseech His grace to expand your heart to receive more of Him.

Memorization Recommended.

The beginning of pride
is man's stubbornness,
he withdraws his heart
from his maker.

- Sirach 10:12

Another incredibly freeing passage! We all know the truth that we do withdraw our hearts from God. The beautiful thing is, to return to God is simply an act of the will, a simple choice. Acknowledge the truth of the areas in your heart and in your life where you have withdrawn from God, walked away from God, the decision to go your own way and not His. Renounce this stubbornness, and turn back to the Lord, He will receive you with open arms.

Memorization Recommended.

I will lead the blind on their journey;
By paths unknown I will guide them.
I will turn darkness into light before them,
And make crooked ways straight.
These things I will do for them,
And I will not forsake them.

- Isaiah 42:16

Are you blind? Do you feel you are living in darkness right now? Pray this passage slowly and imagine yourself in each line of the text. We have all been there, this feeling of wandering without purpose is universal in the human heart because of sin. The last two lines are a proclamation of God's nearness to us and His promises. He will lead us, guide us, light our way, make our path straight and smooth, and He will never, not ever, forsake us. If you are tempted to not believe this passage and the promises of God, renounce the lies of the evil one and be free to receive all that God has for you.

Pray this passage for yourself
and for a loved one that is lost right now.

4

MORAL ACTION

Now that we have praised the Lord, and faced our sin, it's time to ask the question: "How do we go forward in a new life in this new and deeper relationship with the Lord?" Scripture exhorts us to "put on the mind of Christ," it also says that we must "be born of water and the spirit." We know that Jesus "knocks on the door of our heart" and if we answer He will come in and share a meal with us. All of these images from Scripture indicate a totally new way of living. In this chapter we will meditate on passages that tell us exactly what our new life should look like, what we should be striving for in this renewal of our mind, and how to think, act, love through Jesus' own heart.

They are happy whose life is blameless,
who follow God's law!

- Psalm 119:1

We all desire to be happy, but we know we are not blameless, and part of not being blameless is that we don't follow God's law all the time. Let's start with God's law, there are many misconceptions about it. Think of the 10 commandments, few people would disagree with those. Don't commit adultery, don't steal, don't bear false witness, don't murder. These things are written into human nature and make sense to us. If we all did these things, we would be happier and many people would be happier, think about how high the divorce rate is right now. The truth is that through His law, God is directing us to a happy and a good life. That is the purpose of His law, to tell us, to remind us, to encourage us to act in such a way that we will avoid pain and live happy and joyful lives. So, know God's law and follow it with all your heart!

Memorization Recommended.

Rejoice in hope,

endure in affliction,

persevere in prayer.

- Romans 12:12

This passage is a call to action, even a battle cry! Have we not all experienced affliction? Have we not all found prayer to be difficult or tedious? But here we can make no excuses, if we are in a difficult place, then we should hope in the future with the Lord, and rejoice in it. If affliction is ours today, we must endure, for it will come to an end, that is God's promise. If prayer is unhappy for us right now, we must continue, even double down on it, God's consolation will return.

Ups and downs in the spiritual life are natural.
Don't worry, if things are difficult now,
it means that joy and consolation are close at hand.
Rejoice, endure, and persevere!

What pagans sacrifice,
they offer to demons and not to God.
I do not want you to be
partners with demons.
You cannot drink the cup of the Lord
and the cup of demons.
You cannot partake of the table of the Lord
and the table of demons.

- 1 Corinthians 10:20-21

Today, we do not think of pagans, and we do not think of demons, and we do not think of sacrifice to God or demons. This passage challenges us to recognize the truth of our lives and the world around us. Pagan sacrifice is alive and well, and might take the form of being a workaholic, being an alcoholic, a pornography addict, thinking we are not worthy and never will be, or any number of other modern maladies. Our enemy, the devil, has induced us to believe that these things are just the way life is and are no big deal. In this passage we have the opportunity to face the truth and acknowledge that the father of lies has duped us. This kind of action on his part is in keeping with his character: a liar and the father of lies. The first step to breaking this cycle and being free of the lies we have swallowed is to recognize the lie, renounce it, and take action to step into God's grace, into God's light, and into the love that heals.

Take 10 minutes with Jesus to consider where you have accepted lies from the enemy, renounce those lies, give them to Jesus and ask Him what truths He would like to give you to replace those lies.

Everyone who listens to these

words of mine

and acts on them

is like a wise man who built

his house on rock.

\- Matthew 7:24

There are two steps to enacting this scripture. We must listen to the Lord, and then act on what we hear. Listening to the Lord takes time and practice. You can't listen to anyone without time, and we all know that listening takes practice. How much of what we say and what we hear is misunderstood? Quite a bit if you think about it. Spend time every day listening to God by reading and praying with Scripture, start with 10 minutes a day. You will grow in your confidence in hearing God's voice, and once you know it is the Lord speaking, acting on His tender and loving speech to you becomes so much easier because you have experienced His love firsthand. When we do this, we can be assured that our house is built on rock, meaning our life is built on the rock of God.

Memorization Recommended.

Put on the armor of God
so that you may be able to stand firm
against the tactics of the devil.

- Ephesians 6:11

The devil is real, and his tactics are real. Remember when you were a little child and someone shared with you the image of an angel on each shoulder? One was your guardian angel, the other, your personal little demon. This is not like the tooth fairy, this is actually real. Think about when you experience temptation, whose voice do you hear? It is your personal little demon enticing you. The armor of God is truth, righteousness, the gospel, faith, salvation, and prayer. In Ephesians chapter 6 verses 12 through 20, it describes in detail this armor of God.

The phrase "tactics of the devil" indicates the
true battle that we are in.
Arm yourselves for battle with prayer and faith.

Evil men leave the straight paths

to walk in ways of darkness.

- Proverbs 2:13

Do not fellowship with darkness, do not fellowship with evil men. Stay on the straight path of fellowship with Jesus Christ. The world wants to entice you that its path is the most titillating, engaging, and exotic. The world wants to make you think that God's straight path is boring and vanilla. Nothing could be further from the truth. To step into God's plan for your life is the most exciting, fulfilling, joyful, peaceful, amazing thing that you will ever experience this side of heaven. Have compassion on evil men and pray for them, for they are sad men wandering and lost in darkness.

Commit to the straight path of the Lord,
commit your life to Him every day.

Wisdom will enter your heart,
discretion will watch over you,
saving you from the way of evil men.

- Proverbs 2:10

You may think that wisdom is not for you, but God promises wisdom to you here. Wisdom helps us to know in what way to walk, how to direct our life, what to do in a specific situation. If you have never prayed for wisdom, look at a decision that you need to make in the next day or two and ask God for wisdom about that decision. When He answers your prayer, there is so much joy! And if He does not answer, it means He trusts your judgment and He is with you. One definition of discretion is "the freedom to decide what should be done in a particular situation." In this passage God promises that discretion will watch over you, meaning, it will guide you, be with you, and help you. The purpose of wisdom and discretion in this passage is to save you from the ways of evil men. Praise God for wisdom and discretion!

Declare this passage to yourself and
ask Wisdom to enter your heart today.

All things are lawful,

but not all things are helpful.

All things are lawful,

but not all things build up.

- 1 Corinthians 10:23

This is an interesting passage today. So many things are lawful in our society but go against God's law. For us, we want to ask what is truly helpful in our life, and what truly builds us up? These are the things we should be focused on, be growing in our lives and in the lives of those we love.

Speak encouraging words to someone today,
words that will help, encourage and build them up.

By Baptism,

we were buried with Christ into his death,

so that as Christ was raised from the dead

by the glory of the Father,

we too might walk in newness of life.

- Romans 6:4

Baptism is a wonderful thing to study and meditate on. In the early Church Baptism was full immersion. Candidates would enter a pool on one side, be fully immersed, stand up and walk out the other side of the pool. This was to represent death, by being under the water and secondly leaving the pool on the other side represented totally and completely new life in Christ. We also know that in Baptism we are adopted into the family of God, and Christ becomes our brother. So, we know that if the glory of God the Father raised Christ from the dead, we also will be raised by the glory of the Father. We don't often think of these lofty things, but the fact is they are true. And to know these things in the depths of your being and to live them every day will change your life.

Take a day this week to meditate on Baptism all day!

Listen to my voice,

then I will be your God

and you shall be my people.

- Jeremiah 7:23

Our modern ear does not like the "listen to my voice" that begins this passage. We like to go our own way, do our own thing, and be free in that sense. This demonstrates how tainted we are by the world, the flesh, and the devil, the primary temptations to sin. The truth is, the voice of the Lord is love, compassion, mercy, peace and joy. God is simply stating here that those who listen to His voice are His people, those who do not listen to His voice have chosen to not be in relationship with Him. That is how real and strong and free we actually are, we can say no to God and it sticks. Let us not exercise our freedom in that way. But let us joyfully listen to the voice of our loving God and continue to entrust our lives to Him.

Listen to God's voice today, He is always,
at every moment, pouring His love out to you.

But as for us, the Lord is our God,
and we have not forsaken him.

- 2 Chronicles 13:10

This is a marvelous passage to encourage us to never forsake Him. He never forsakes us, and *by His grace* we can return the favor. When faced with temptation, you can quote this passage, remain firm in the Lord, and the enemy will take flight.

Memorization Recommended.

Your all-powerful word,
from heaven's royal throne,
bounded into the land,
bearing the sharp sword
of your inexorable decree.

- Wisdom 18:15-16

What is God's "inexorable decree"? Inexorable means something that is impossible to stop or prevent. God's decree is love and salvation, and it is impossible to stop because it has already been poured out, it is currently being poured out, and it will always be poured out. It is a sharp sword because some refuse to accept His love and salvation. But look where this decree comes from, "His all powerful word" which is Jesus Christ. Christ and His word originate from heaven's royal throne which happens to be our destiny! The phrase "bounding into the land" can be seen as the stunning unfolding of creation and the splendor of the universe pressing in on us with all its beauty. This is God, sharing with us the abundance of His goodness, beauty, joy and His longing for us to receive His salvation, love and peace.

Spend some minutes imagining God's Word,
originating from the throne room,
bounding into your life.

I am the true vine and my Father
is the vine dresser.
Every branch of mine that bears no fruit,
He takes away,
and every branch that does bear fruit
He prunes, that it may bear more fruit.

- John 15:1-2

Most Christians are quite familiar with this image. Jesus is the vine and we are the branches. First, it is important to remain on the vine, do not knowingly cut yourself off from Jesus. Now we have the question of fruit. Is my life bearing fruit? Is your life bearing fruit? How to measure the fruit, how to gauge it? It is important to know that we must remain in God and God in us, because truly the fruit is His; we are simply instruments, we are clay in the Potters hand, that is how we participate in the bringing forth of the Kingdom here on earth. Never forget it is His Kingdom, not ours. The take away for this passage is that even if we are bearing fruit the Father will prune us so that we can produce more fruit. Pruning a tree or pruning my life is a painful process. Things are cut off. There are parts of my life that are not beneficial for me, or for bearing fruit for the Kingdom of God. Let us give God permission to prune us today, to cut away from our life that which is not life-giving.

Dear Father in heaven,
I give you permission to prune me today.

I beseech, you by the mercies of God,
to present your bodies as a living sacrifice,
holy and acceptable to God,
which is your spiritual worship.
Do not be conformed to this present world
but be transformed by
the renewal of your mind,
that you may know what is the will of God,
what is good, acceptable, and perfect.

- Romans 12:1-2

This dense passage presents us with another unbelievable principle of the Christian life: that we may know the very will of God by the renewal of our own mind. In the New Testament we are told quite a number of times that we are to put on the mind of Christ. How many of us take God at His word and invite Jesus in to transform our very thinking. Perhaps a simple human analogy will help. After many years of loving marriage, spouses can easily finish each other's sentences, they can anticipate their needs and wants. If this can occur over the course of years of loving fellowship between human beings, how much more so can our mind become one with Christ's mind when He states His intention to have this type of fellowship with us.

To enter into the renewal of your mind in earnest, ask Jesus what He thinks about such and such or so and so, and then listen for His answer.

5

COMFORT & CONSOLATION

The comfort and consolation of God Himself in our life is like no other. He created us and knows us better than we know ourselves. He knows all of our wounds, He knows all of our hurts, He knows what inspires us, He knows what brings us joy, He knows what frustrates us, and He knows what makes us laugh! To be comforted and consoled by God is to be loved by your best friend in every situation of your life. If Jesus is not your best friend yet, perhaps He will be by the end of this chapter!

The Lord God will wipe away
the tears from all faces.

- Isaiah 25:8

This is a wonderfully consoling passage and also
a challenging one. That God desires to wipe the
tears from our faces is a great joy and expresses the
tenderness of His love towards us. That he doesn't
wipe them away simultaneously to my shedding them
is difficult, and tests my faith. Yet we all know that
sadness and tears are part of life and also take time.
In grieving the loss of a loved one tears don't go away
overnight, in grieving the loss of a job that you loved,
that also does not go away overnight. That Jesus
himself shed tears at the death of Lazarus shows us that
He understands our sorrow and all kinds of different
sorrows. Rest in the tenderness of God's desire to wipe
your tears away. For He will surely do so.

Chat with Jesus about a long ago sorrow and
ask Him to show you how He was present when that
sorrow occurred.

Memorization Recommended.

The Lord will give strength to his people,
the Lord will bless his people with peace.

- Psalm 29:11

Strength and peace are the Lords to give. We have our own version of strength and peace, but it is a million orders of magnitude different from God's. Don't forget, this is the guy who created everything that exists in the entire universe just by speaking a few words. Again, we run into the unimaginable. A statement of God that He will actually impart His strength and His peace (He is not simply talking about augmenting our own, but giving some of His own). For many of us, unbelief lurks under the surface. It's a pretty passage, it's a nice passage, it rolls off the tongue. But the truth is, that in our hearts, there is unbelief. Today let us unmask that unbelief and take its power away by declaring the truth.

Memorization Recommended.

For us, he became poor,

that by his poverty,

we might become rich.

- 2 Corinthians 8:9

The poverty of Jesus is demonstrated in the Incarnation. He divested Himself of the glory of being God so that He could walk among us. By doing this, He Himself becomes the bridge to *our divinization.* By our Baptism we are adopted into the family of God and Jesus is our brother. You will hear later about the Holy Spirit being the first installment of our inheritance. The richness that we are to gain is becoming a member of the family of God. Imagine how your life would change if you were adopted into the family of a millionaire or billionaire. The adoption into God's family and becoming rich with God is of an entirely different type and magnitude. Its scope is eternal, its depth is infinite. The richness that is ours is beyond our imagining. I encouraged you to expand your mind and heart about what riches the Lord has that He would like to pour into your life.

Ask God what riches He desires to pour
into your life today.

These things I have spoken to you,

that my joy may be in you,

and that your joy may be full.

- John 15:11

In this passage, Jesus is the one who is speaking. This is in John's gospel shortly before the Passion. This is a time when He is sharing His last thoughts with His apostles and followers. He is speaking very plainly because He knows the challenges they will face in the next days. He promises His joy, He desires that their hearts be full of joy, and He is also speaking to us, that our hearts would be filled with joy. Joy is often hard to come by in this world, but for followers of Jesus, we have an inside track! Remember, this is a joy that the world does not know, cannot give, and cannot take away.

Memorization Recommended.

You nourished your people
with the food of angels,
furnished them with bread from heaven,
ready to hand, untoiled for,
endowed with all delights,
and conforming to every taste.

- Wisdom 16:20

To plumb the depths of this passage, we need to understand analogy, and food and nourishment. All areas of our life require nourishment. We need air to breathe, we need food to eat, we need rest, we need happiness and peace and excitement and joy and friends and contentment and more. All of these things nourish us. Carefully note the qualities of the nourishment God offers: it comes from heaven, it is fully prepared for us and ready to consume, it is untoiled for, meaning no work required, it is free to us. The bread He gives contains all delights, that's right ALL delights. And lastly, it conforms to every taste, it is perfectly and personally suited to each of us. Talk about a gourmet meal!!! This nourishment is like no other, it will sustain us through all of life, through the most difficult challenges, as well as accompanying us in life's joys, and it will bring us to rest in the Father's arms at the end of our days. Be sure to always have some of this bread on hand, you don't want to be without it.

Ask God to nourish you with some of this bread today! Memorization Recommended.

*We who live are constantly
being given up to death
for the sake of Jesus,
so that the life of Jesus may be
manifested in our mortal flesh.*

- 2 Corinthians 4:11

Jesus told His followers that the world would reject Him and would also reject us. This is one aspect of "being given up to death for the sake of Jesus." The world has rejected Jesus, but we have not. We have accepted Him. He is our Savior. As we experience tribulation in this life, we are united to Jesus in His Passion. In this passage Jesus promises that His life will be manifested in us, in our flesh, and in our bodies. What does this mean? It means that the life of Jesus will be re-lived in us: in our hearts, in our minds, in our bodies, and in our life. This only occurs if we allow Him to live in us. Ask yourself, what aspect of Christ's life is He asking you to live right now? Are you at Bethlehem with the holy family? Are you with Him in His hidden life before public ministry? Are you working miracles with Him? Are you in the Paschal Mystery with Him right now? Are you in the tomb? Or at the Resurrection? Trust that He will shine forth from us so that others may live. The life of Christ is present in us in order to convert the nations. Do you see your life in this light? This is the light of Jesus, this is the light of faith, this is the light that we are called to shine into a dark world.

Memorization Recommended.

Brothers and sisters,

draw strength from the Lord

and from his mighty power.

- Ephesians 6:10

Once again we see God promising to give us His very own strength and power. I encourage you to meditate on various things that His power has done: creation, Moses and Aaron's miracles before pharaoh, parting the Red Sea, lighting the fire of Elijah's sacrifice after hundreds of gallons of water were poured on the wood, and a virgin birth just to name a few. In the New Testament we see God sharing His mighty power with the apostles and all of His followers. He had given them authority and they went out and cast out demons, healed the sick, and preached the Kingdom. His power is real, and He does share it with us. Why wouldn't He share it with His very own sons and daughters? How are you in touch with His mighty power in your life?

Memorization Recommended.

I have been crucified with Christ,

yet I live, no longer I,

but Christ lives in me.

- Galatians 2:19

To be crucified with Christ means many different things. First it means Baptism, secondly it means the daily crucifixion of being a Christian in a world that rejects Jesus. The good news is, through Baptism, Jesus now lives in me and in you, and we together make up the body of Christ in the world today. Do you visit with the one who has taken up residence in your heart? Do you visit with Him every day? Do you consult Him throughout the day? Do you reflect with Him at the end of the day about how the day went? I encourage you to not ignore the roommate of your heart!

Memorization Recommended.

I tell you the truth,
it is to your advantage that I go away,
for if I do not go away
the Counselor will not come to you.
But if I go, I will send him to you.

- John 16:7

It is good that Jesus said this out loud. The apostles and disciples traveled with Jesus and lived with him intimately for three years. They saw all of His miracles, they saw the casting out of demons, they saw lives changed, they saw Him be rejected by many. This is the place in John's gospel where He is preparing them for His departure. Sometimes the word "Counselor" is translated as "Advocate," in this sense it means one who will strengthen and defend in a legal sense. Either way, the Holy Spirit will be with them in a way that they do not understand right now. Have we received the baptism in the Holy Spirit that scripture often speaks about? We are not meant to live this life without the Holy Spirit. Jesus specifically wanted the Holy Spirit to be with us once He left. We also know that we are to grow in the spiritual life, just like we saw the apostles grow throughout the New Testament. After Pentecost, they grew in their intimacy with the Holy Spirit and in their cooperation with the action of the Holy Spirit, and so must we. With God, there is always more. More Holy Spirit please!

Ask for a greater outpouring of the Holy Spirit in your life!

The hour is coming, indeed it has come,
when you will be scattered,
every man to his home
and you will leave me alone.
Yet I am not alone,
for the Father is with me.
I have said this to you,
that in me you may have peace.
In the world you have tribulation,
but be of good cheer,
I have overcome the world!

- John 16: 32-33

Jesus is telling us here that He understands the feeling of being alone. And He buoys us up by sharing that He is not alone and that we are never alone. In our loneliness, in that place where we feel unloved, He is pouring out the salve of His presence and His peace. Once again this is His peace, a peace that the world does not know, cannot give, and cannot take away. He recognizes our tribulation and comforts us with the truth that He has already overcome the world. We can rejoice that we are His and He is ours.

Use this passage as a declaration,
reminding yourself that Jesus has indeed
overcome the world, the salvation of the human race
is already accomplished!

Peace, I leave with you,

my peace, I give to you,

not as the world gives do I give to you.

Let not your hearts be troubled,

neither let them be afraid.

- John 14:27

Peace is a frequent theme for Jesus. He knows that our hearts trouble easily, and we need peace, and more peace, and even more peace. The last sentence of this passage is given to us as an imperative, that means it is given to us as a command. He is commanding us to not be troubled or afraid. This is the perfect kind of passage that we use as a declaration, we come into agreement with it and when necessary, we cast out fear in the name of Jesus.

Memorization Recommended.

In my father's house are many rooms,

if it were not so, would I have told you

that I go to prepare a place for you?

And when I go and prepare a place for you,

I will come again and will

take you to myself,

that where I am you may also be.

- John 14:2-3

This is a lovely passage for those who are not sure about heaven. Let's remember that in the Christian Creed we say "I believe in God the Father, creator of heaven and earth." So, heaven is a place, and as Jesus was resurrected so will we be resurrected, in our bodies. Heaven is often described as a banquet, or a wedding feast. So, it certainly is a physical place, but glorified bodies are quite different from our earthly bodies. Just spend a little time studying the resurrection appearances of Jesus at the end of each of the four Gospels.

Spend some time with Jesus imaging
about the place He is preparing for you.

6

TRIBULATION & HOPE

Jesus told his followers many times that the world hates Him, and the world would hate them. He also spoke plainly about taking up their own cross and following Him. The Christian life doesn't smell like roses all the time. The fact is, we are soldiers on a battlefield, and the sooner we understand the nature of the battle, and the nature of our enemy, the sooner we will be able to fully engage in the battle. But let's remember, the victory is already won. What we are doing in this life could be considered mop up activities. Jesus put sin to death once and for all on the Cross. By His blood we are saved. Now that we have been comforted and consoled, it is time to face tribulation in our life and how we should respond to it.

I pour out my troubles before him,

I tell him all my distress

while my spirit faints within me.

But you, Oh Lord, know my path.

- Psalm 142:2-3

We have no need to fear God. He wants us to share with Him all of our troubles, all of our distress, all of our anxieties, all of our fears, everything that causes our spirits to faint. Many people would object, saying, God knows all these things. And they would be right. The difference is when we actively tell Him all of these things, we are signaling to God that we want a relationship with Him, we are signaling that we want Him to know all these things. If we don't tell Him in our own words what is in our heart, He knows it, but not by friendship, He would know it by being God and the one who created us and knows us more intimately than we know ourselves. To open our heart to the Lord signals that we want an intimate friendship with Him. In addition to all of that, after I share all of my distress and troubles with Him, He knows my path! He assures me that He knows my path, and is with me in walking that path. He is my constant companion all because I poured out my troubles to Him.

Take 5 minutes and pour out your troubles to the Lord.
Memorization Recommended.

Over all people
his glory will be shelter and protection:
shade from the parching heat of day,
refuge and cover from storm and rain.

- Isaiah 4:6

His glory will be our shelter and protection. Think about that. What does God's glory as shelter and protection look like? It protects us from the heat of day, or perhaps the heat of battle. It protects us from storm and rain, what kinds of storms? What kinds of rain? The storms of life are many and varied. Rain comes sometimes when least expected. Imagine God's glory guarding you in these situations. The next time the heat of battle, a storm of life, or sorrow rains down on you, conjure up this image of glory over you protecting you, and loving you.

Pray for the shelter and protection of God's glory
to be upon someone you know who is in a battle,
battered by a storm, or immersed in sorrow.

Memorization Recommended.

Before they call, I will answer,
while they are yet speaking, I will hear.

- Isaiah 65:24

How comforting that God always hears me, and that He knows the answer even before I ask the question. For us, time is a conundrum. We live in the present, and often the past dominates our mind, or we are obsessed with controlling the future. But for God, time is unrolled before Him, and every moment of time is in the present tense. Before I call out to Him, He knows how He will comfort me, guide me, pour out His wisdom into me, and love me through my current difficulty. That is why I called out to Him in the first place! What a joy that the God of the universe hears little old me!

Memorization Recommended.

Everyone in the crowd sought to touch him because power came forth from him and healed them all.

- Luke 6:19

That's right, He healed them all. It makes sense that everyone in the crowd sought to touch him. I would too. Do you believe that He heals even today? I encourage you to think about what wound in your life you would like Jesus to heal today. Jesus is as alive today as He was when He walked the earth, and He gave us His Holy Spirit to teach us, to remind us of everything that Jesus taught us, and to convey the power and the love of God in our lives right now. Present to God the wound of your heart, or a physical wound and ask Him to heal it today.

Use this passage as a declaration to drive out unbelief and let Jesus begin healing in your life today!

Memorization Recommended.

I cry to you Oh Lord. You are my refuge,
all I have left in the land of the living.
Listen, then, to my cry
for I am in the depths of distress.

- Psalm 124:5-6

Here we are given permission to cry out to the Lord in the depths of our distress. There is nothing and nowhere that can separate us from the love of God. Do not be ashamed of being in the depths of distress, we live in a world dominated by sin, and the battle rages for our soul and for the souls of all the living. Cry out to the Lord and be assured of an attentive ear. What a gift this passage is for all believers. For those who do not know the Lord, they do not know that He is a sure refuge, they simply do not have a refuge. They must face their distress alone. But not us, and we need to share this good news. For it truly and surely is good news!

Memorization recommended
and share this good news!

Cease your cries of mourning,

wipe the tears from your eyes.

The sorrow you have shown

shall have its reward.

- Jeremiah 31:16

How does sorrow have a reward? It is because your heart has gone out to another. You have shown compassion, tender compassion. And we know that the Lord wipes away every tear from our eyes, and turns our mourning into joy. There is a time for mourning and a time for tears, and a time to wipe away those tears.

Spend some time praying for,
and lifting up to the throne of grace,
a friend who mourns.

Rejoice in the Lord always;
again, I say, Rejoice!
... Have no anxiety about anything,
but in everything by prayer
and supplication,
with thanksgiving,
let your requests be made known to God.
And the peace of God,
which passes all understanding,
will guard your hearts
and minds in Christ Jesus.

- Philippians 4:4, 6-7

This is a passage to enact phrase by phrase. We begin by rejoicing. Don't skip that step. And then we have an imperative, He gives us a command to have no anxiety about anything. This is a difficult command. And the language is clear, NO ANXIETY about ANYTHING. The beautiful thing is, then He tells us how to accomplish this. We begin by prayer and supplication, that means begging God. Then we thank God. Perhaps we thank Him for the gift of faith, perhaps we thank Him for the gift of prayer, perhaps we thank Him for remembering this passage and to enact this method. Then we make our request known to God, simply and clearly. After all of that, the peace of God will come to us to literally guard our heart and our mind. The peace of God is an active force that shields our heart and mind in Christ Jesus and protects us from anxiety. Praise the Lord!

Memorization Recommended.

For as the heavens are higher than the earth,

so my ways higher than your ways,

my thoughts higher than your thoughts.

- Isaiah 55:9

When I am at the end of my rope, when I think there is no way out, I recite this passage. It reminds me that I'm not the smartest person in the room. It reminds me to ask for God's wisdom. It reminds me that life is so much bigger than my current circumstances. It reminds me that God has a plan and all I need to do is lean into it. Lord, teach me your thoughts and your ways.

Memorization recommended

For you shall go out in joy
and be led forth in peace.

- Isaiah 55:12

I definitely want to be led into this passage. That the Lord would take me by the hand and lead me into peace and that He would send me out into the world with joy is such a comforting thought. Again, we run into unbelief. Proclaim this passage out loud and let the Lord surprise you with joy and peace, for He has promised it. He is trustworthy and He will do it. Alleluia!

Memorization Recommended

I rejoice in my sufferings for your sake,
in my flesh I am filling up what is lacking
in the afflictions of Christ,
on behalf of his body the Church.

- Colossians 1:24

Rejoicing in my sufferings, hmm that doesn't sound right. Is something lacking in Christ's afflictions? I don't think so. What could this possibly mean? We do know that Jesus invited us to take up our cross and follow Him. It means that each one of us has our own cross. Jesus had a big one, we have a little one in comparison. Though most of the time it doesn't feel little. So, He has given us a way to rejoice in our sufferings. It is called uniting our sufferings to His. This gives our suffering meaning. Jesus conquered sin and put death itself to death. When we unite our sufferings to His, our burden becomes lighter (as He promised) and we participate in the very work of Christ. It is a mystery, no doubt. But no less true and real because of its mysteriousness. As for what might be lacking in the sufferings of Christ, there is only one thing. What is lacking is simply the application of Jesus' merits and work of salvation to the life of each and every person. This application and reception of Christ's salvation to each life happens in time. I didn't live when Christ walked the earth, so I need to receive the gift of salvation here, and now, in my life in the 21st century. So do you, and so does the whole world. We can join in the work of Jesus by lifting up our sufferings and uniting them to Jesus' own suffering and asking Him to prepare hearts to receive the Good News of salvation.

Memorization Recommended

I will pour water upon the thirsty ground,

and streams upon the dry land.

- Isaiah 44:3

Is He talking about drought here? I don't think so. The thirsty ground and the dry land is my heart and your heart. The question is, is your heart thirsty? We want to be thirsty for the Lord. If we are too dry the rain, that is the grace, will pour right over us and run off and we won't be able to receive it. We want to both be thirsty and be able to receive the streams of His grace, His very life. Fix your eyes on the Lord and never, not ever, take your eyes off of Him. And when He pours water onto your thirsty heart you will be able to take it in. This water will refresh you, it will cleanse you, it will bring you wisdom, joy and fellowship with Him.

Memorization recommended

7

HAVE NO FEAR

Scripture contains the phrase "have no fear," or "fear not," 365 times. That seems to me to be at least one per day, every day, all year long, every year!! We need to be reminded of this often, because fear has not been cast out of our hearts yet. Let us distinguish between the two major types of fear. One, is fear of the Lord, and that is the overwhelming experience of the awesomeness and glory and love of God. This is the fear that is the beginning of wisdom. The second major type of fear is a fear that is caused by lack of trust in God, it is primary a tactic of the enemy. Once we understand this tactic of the enemy, and we have beefed up our faith and our trust, then truly we have nothing to fear!

Praise the Lord!

Fear not, for I have redeemed you.
I have called you by name, you are mine.

- Isaiah 43:1

I believe that Scripture tells us to "fear not" 365 times, it seems to me there is one for each day of the year. And yet, we still fear. In this instance, God gives us a reason, we don't have to fear because He has redeemed us. But what is redemption? In the simplest terms, we have been purchased. We were slaves, and given over to our enemy, the liar and father of lies. By the blood of Jesus, we have been freed by God. God paid the price and we received the reward. That reward is hinted at in the second line of this passage. God has called us by name, He knows us by name, and we are His. We are His not in a possessive sense, but by way of infinite love and communion that will take an eternity to enter into once we get to heaven. But of course, we can begin that loving communion here on earth!

Memorization recommended

Bring my sons from afar,
and my daughters from
the ends of the earth.
Everyone who is called by my name,
whom I created for my glory,
whom I formed and made.

- Isaiah 43:6-7

This passage makes me think of my sons and daughters who are far from the Lord. God created each individual uniquely and beautifully and to be part of His plan in the unfolding of His Kingdom here on this earth. He calls each of us by name to participate in His glory. God's Providence is drawing all to Himself. Our sons and daughters are included in His plan, as are all of those dear to us. Take heart, He is calling all of us by name. Open the ears of your heart to hear His beautiful call to you.

Memorization recommended
and share this passage with a friend.

When you pass through the waters
I will be with you,
and through the rivers,
they shall not overwhelm you.
When you walk through fire
you shall not be burned,
and the flame shall not consume you.
For I am the Lord your God
the holy one of Israel, your Savior.

- Isaiah 43:2-3

In scripture, water and fire are often used as images of the Holy Spirit. Here these images are used in a natural sense, waters that drown, and fires that destroy. These are powerful images especially if you have ever experienced a devastating flood or forest fire where you lost a home or an entire community. We can also easily imagine the tragedies of life, the sudden loss of a loved one, the sudden onset of a debilitating injury or illness, or the depression and anxiety which is so common in modern life. We are assured here that the Lord our God is with us and is saving us.

Memorization recommended

Take care,

be earnestly on your guard

not to forget

the things which your own eyes have seen,

nor let them slip from your memory.

As long as you live,

teach them to your children

and grandchildren.

- Deuteronomy 4:9

You are Christian for a reason, think about and call to mind all the things you have seen with your own eyes in terms of God loving you and those around you. We should recall these things often. We should not forget God's kindness, mercy, and love towards us. In teaching our children about God, we should often bear witness to the work of God in our own life. It will bring God and His love alive to them. Bearing witness to others also keeps alive in our own mind all that God has done for us.

Share with someone the Good News
of Jesus Christ today!
Memorization Recommended.

Truly, truly, I say to you,

you will weep and lament,

and the world will rejoice.

You will be sorrowful,

but your sorrow will be turned to joy.

- John 16:20

Let us never forget that the world in which we live is at odds with our Savior. When Jesus was going to the cross, even His apostles abandoned Him. The truth is we would have as well. And the world at the time, the Romans, actually did rejoice at His death. But as often happens in the Christian life, things are not as they seem. The apostles and disciples were sorrowful, and their sorrow did turn to joy at the Resurrection. And so will ours. That is His promise to us.

Memorization recommended

Let our sacrifice be in your presence today
as we follow you unreservedly.
For those who trust in you
cannot be put to shame,
and now we follow you with
our whole heart,
we fear you, and we pray to you.

- Daniel 3:39-41

To follow God unreservedly means to give your life as a sacrifice to Him, and to hold nothing back. This means we give Him our whole heart, everyday and without reservation. This is a scary thing because here on this earth, with people, that is a hard thing to do because people are sinful (we are sinful!). And they will always hurt us in one way or another, sooner or later. But God is different, He is without sin, He is all goodness, He will never betray us. So we can trust completely and unreservedly in placing our life and our heart in his hands, they will be safe. We fear Him with a holy fear. This kind of fear is a biblical fear that acknowledges the beauty and glory of God, in the presence of which we are awestruck. This is true fear of the Lord, because He is glorious to behold.

Memorization recommended,
focusing especially on giving ourselves unreservedly.

I pummel my body and subdue it,

lest after preaching to others

I, myself, should be disqualified.

- 1 Corinthians 9:27

Paul is encouraging us here to enter into bodily penance. He recognizes that even though he is a gifted preacher, by the gift of God, that he could fall away. One tried and true method to keep the evil one at bay is to practice bodily penance. Because of original sin, our bodies are in rebellion, my body always wants a third piece of chocolate cake, or a second bowl of ice cream. It is rebellion against the rule of my mind, it is rebellion against moderation. It simply wants its own way and it wants that chocolate cake and that second bowl of ice cream. To discipline ourselves in our body, will assist in the discipline of our mind and our heart. Even Paul, the great preacher that he was, practiced bodily penance. If it's good enough for him, it certainly is good enough for me, how about you?

Choose a penance to do for the rest of the day.
Fast from social media, go to bed earlier like you have been planning to, have a second helping of those dreaded green beans... be creative!

8

WISDOM

Many people think Biblical wisdom is not for them. This is another lie from the enemy. What is biblical wisdom? Many of us could not even answer that question. So, if we're not sure what it is, why would we think it is not for us? In its simplest and most common form, Biblical wisdom is how a Godly person would act in any given circumstance. When we face a conundrum, something that we can't quite figure out, or don't know how to do or act, it may be a relationship issue, a work issue, a decision that we need to make that we are unsure of how to proceed. This is when we should seek out heavenly Wisdom. Wisdom knows the way out, Wisdom knows the solution, wisdom was with God before the creation of the world, and God has clearly stated that He wants to share Wisdom with us and wants Wisdom to be our dear, dear friend.

Let my instruction soak in like the rain,

my discourse permeate like the dew.

- Deuteronomy 32:2

The speaker here is God himself. The images He is using to teach us are so gentle, and so organic. His teaching, it's like rain that the ground soaks up and loves. It is a soil that is rich, a soil that is fertile, a soil that is ready to grow whatever seeds are planted. The action of soil receiving water in a soaking rain is natural and easy. The instruction of the Lord is the rain, and the soil that receives it is our heart. We need to be sure that our heart is prepared to naturally, easily, and readily receive the instruction that God sends our way. God is also the sower, He sows seeds in our heart and we need to let them grow, usually these seeds are related to the unfolding of His Kingdom here in this life. When it comes to God's discourse, these are conversations a little bit longer, with the Lord. Think of a complex lecture that you heard in college or listening to a TedX talk, or something like that, that was intriguing, but deep, and new ideas that you weren't familiar with were presented. This type of discourse takes some time to permeate and percolate in our souls. The Lord also speaks to us in this way with more complex topics, more complex ideas, and certainly God thinks outside the box and encourages us too as well.

Next time it rains, think of this passage.
Memorization Recommended.

Who has cupped the wind in his hands?

Who has bound up the waters in a cloak?

What is his name? What is his son's name?

Every word of the Lord is tested;

He is a shield

to those who take refuge in him.

- Proverbs 30:4-5

This passage is evocative of creation. Certainly it is the Lord who has cupped the wind in His hands and bound up the waters in His cloak. What is His name? Yahweh. What is His son's name? Jesus. The Lord is not afraid of every word of His being tested. For every word is true and worthy of belief. Having made the world, and everything in it, He indeed is a shield for those of us who take refuge in Him.

Never be afraid to take refuge in Him.
Or, in other words, take refuge in Him often!

He who fashioned the heart of each,

he who knows all their works.

- Psalm 33:15

This is a tricky one. Some of us, many of us, are not happy at this moment about how God has fashioned our heart. We need to make an inquiry about this. God does not make mistakes. He fashioned each one of us, and our hearts out of love and for love. So, cast aside unbelief, dig deep, and look at your wounds, and present them to the Lord for healing, and proclaim the truth that God created your heart for love, and to fill your heart with His love.

Present your heart to the Lord,
give it to Him for a software update,
and watch the efficiency of your love fly!!

Memorization Recommended.

Send forth Wisdom from your holy heaven,
and from your throne of glory send her.
That she may work with me,
that I may learn what is pleasing to you,
for she knows and understands all things
and will guide me wisely in all my ways
and guard me with her glory.

- Wisdom 9:10-11

For most people, we don't think we are the ones for wisdom. We just think, that's for someone else, someone better than me, someone smarter than me, someone holier than me. This is simply not true. Scripture teaches us to seek after wisdom. This passage beautifully tells us where wisdom comes from, how she wants to be with us, and the many benefits she desires to bestow upon us. What comfort there is in the proclamation that she will guard me with her glory. I encourage you to ask for wisdom in your everyday life. If you are unsure how to move forward with a work situation, if you are struggling with a child and a difficult situation, if you are unsure how to navigate a conflict with a sibling or a friend, let wisdom be your guide. Ask specific questions for guidance in this situation or that. And then be attentive in you're listening.

Today or tomorrow, seek the guidance of Wisdom.

For us there is one God, the Father,
from whom all things are
and for whom we exist,
and one Lord, Jesus Christ,
through whom all things are
and through whom we exist.

- 1 Corinthians 8:6

What a joy when God speaks so clearly to us, and about such deep topics. The Father is the ground of our existence, He is our origin. We exist because He longed to share Himself and the goodness of Himself. We are the being into which He pours Himself and longs to pour Himself even more. Jesus Christ is the one through whom we exist. That means our every breath, our every thought (which is in words), should praise Him. He is the living Word of God, in which all things are and exist. What does it mean for us to exist in Him? Let this "instruction soak in like the rain, and permeate like the dew," and it will bear much fruit.

Ask Jesus to explain this passage to you.

Thus says the Lord who made you,
who formed you from the womb
and will help you: fear not!

- Isaiah 44:2

Again we are encouraged to 'fear not'. Why would
we ever fear the one who formed us from our very
beginning? There is so much self loathing out there in
the world today. We need to reject this. God loved us into
creation, He loved us into redemption and salvation, and
He loves us through our glorification to heaven. We are
lovable. We need to reject self loathing, and 'fear not' just
as He directs us. We must enter into the truth of who
we are. We are sons and daughters of God the Father,
brothers and sisters of Jesus Christ, and loved beyond our
wildest dreams.

Memorization Recommended.

9

SEEK THE LORD

In the Christian life, it is an assumption that we seek the Lord. Many of us, though, fall away from active seeking. We think once we know Him and He knows us and we are saved, that's pretty much it. This is yet another lie of the enemy. In John chapter 14 and 15 and elsewhere in scripture, God tells us that Jesus and the Father and the Spirit will come and make their home in us. How does that work? An infinite God coming to live in the heart of a finite and sinful creature. This seems the most impossible conundrum. And yet God states it again and again in His holy Word. So, let us wipe away unbelief, and declare these truths to ourselves and to the world. We need to recommit ourselves to always seeking the Lord, because He is always pursuing us and always has more for us!

*That I may know him
and the power of his resurrection.*

- Philippians 3:10

God is trustworthy, right? So, this passage before us, it must mean that you and I are capable of knowing Him and capable of some relationship with the power of His resurrection. I hesitate and say 'some relationship' because the power of His resurrection is a bit daunting to me. This is a passage meant for us to memorize, flat out believe, and live in the deepest way possible. He is constantly resurrecting us, saving us, comforting us, pouring out His grace, mercy, love, joy, and peace upon us. The power of His resurrection is as alive today as it was at the moment of His resurrection 2000 years ago. This is a true statement. If we really believed this, we would shout it from the rooftops. I don't see or hear anybody shouting from the rooftops. We need to realign our lives. We need to align them with the Truth of God, and not the truth of the world. Jesus' resurrection, and its power, are available to us today, tomorrow, and forever. Let's figure out how we can shout it from the rooftops. Will that mean bearing witness to the gospel to a friend, neighbor, or coworker? Will that mean adding "Praise God!" to your everyday vocabulary? As you come "to know Him and the power of His resurrection", this will come into greater focus.

Memorization recommended,
and repeat it often throughout the day.

Let the hearts that seek the Lord rejoice,

turn to the Lord and his strength,

constantly seek his face!

- Psalm 105:3b-4

I think all we have to do here is make sure we are always seeking the Lord and rejoicing in Him!! The eyes of our heart should never leave Him. Did you know that our heart and soul have parallel senses to our body? The five physical senses: sight, smell, taste, hearing, and touch are all replicated in our heart. That means, we have spiritual sight, spiritual smell, spiritual taste, spiritual hearing, and spiritual touch. How does God convey to you, in a sensate experience, His presence? Is it by touch? Is it by sight? Is it by hearing? Let us constantly seek Him, and may our spiritual senses be attentive to His presence.

Memorization Recommended.

God is a deliverer and savior,

working signs and wonders

in heaven and on earth.

- Daniel 6:28

Where are all these signs and wonders? We know God is our deliverer and savior, Praise the Lord! But what about signs and wonders? What signs and wonders occur in heaven? We know signs and wonders were present on the earth during Jesus' public ministry. Again, I ask, what about signs and wonders now? We read moments ago, about the power of Jesus' resurrection, and how it is alive and well today. So, we can surmise that signs and wonders on the earth are also alive and well right now. If you have not seen one recently, let us beseech the throne of grace, and ask for a miracle. I dare you to believe!

Proclaim and declare this passage,
and catalog the signs and wonders that follow!

For you are great
and do marvelous deeds,
you who alone are God.

- Psalm 86:10

Dear Lord Jesus, King of the universe, work marvelous deeds in my life! I declare and proclaim that you alone are God and Lord of my life, and I love you.

Memorization Recommended.

I pour water in the desert

and rivers in the wasteland

for my chosen people to drink.

- Isaiah 43:20b

Are you thirsting for God? We should be. You'll notice
He produces water where it is not expected, the desert,
and the wasteland. Never doubt the qualities of this
water. It is a special water. The water of baptism, the
water of new birth. And yes, we are His chosen people,
we are to drink from this stream of life-giving water.
This water that flows from all eternity through the heart
of Christ after the piercing of the soldiers' lance, into our
hearts and into our lives. Receive this water, and drink
deeply, it will well up within you to eternal life.

Spend 10 minutes in thanksgiving
for the life-giving water God has poured into you.
Share this life-giving water with another.

10

ON MISSION

When God pours His own life into us, and we are filled, we are not meant to revel in it and remain alone. The love of God is to be shared with the world. It is to be shouted from the rooftops. We are to do what Jesus did, to seek out the lost and to love them as He did. We were once lost in sin and the Lord loved us to Himself. We should place ourselves at the service of Jesus and become His instrument so that others might know the joy that we do. On your way to heaven, drag as many people with you as you can. The amazing thing is, that Jesus sent the Holy Spirit for us, and the Holy Spirit will prompt us in new and exciting ways of loving our brothers and sisters. Words of knowledge, prophetic words, miracles, all of this is attested to in the New Testament. God himself will show up to bear witness to our testimony and to work wonders in the hearts of His people whom He loves so much! Go on Mission!

For we are God's coworkers.

- 1 Corinthians 3:9

Again, a very straightforward passage. But is it to be believed? How could we be God's coworkers? Why would He need coworkers? How could anyone be worthy to be His coworker? These questions, and similar ones, drive unbelief and a strong dose of unworthiness. Let us banish these objections, and these falsehoods. Jesus redeemed us with His blood. He made us worthy. Our part is to strive to live up to this awesome gift of redemption. We are human, we grow slowly, we take three steps forward and two steps back. But that is OK as long as we keep our eyes fixed on Jesus. I encourage you to declare this passage to yourself often. I'm sure you have heard that we are the hands and feet of Jesus in this world. This is so true, take Jesus with you as you go throughout your day, listen to the Holy Spirit and His promptings, proclaim the Good News as the Spirit directs. If you don't do this, then Jesus will not be proclaimed in your corner of the world. You are God's coworker, He is training you, He is equipping you, and He has already sent you forth. Go bear fruit that will last!

Memorize and proclaim to yourself often.

For the Kingdom of God
does not consist in talk, but in power.

- 1 Corinthians 4:20

When was the last time you experienced the power of God? Knowing things about God, and talking about God, is good. But to know God in the depths of your heart, and *experience for yourself* His gentleness, His tenderness, His compassion, His mercy, and most especially His love, joy, and peace. These experiences change your world, change the world around you, and demonstrate the truth of God. Another expression of God's power in the world today, is the working of signs and wonders right before our very eyes. Even if you have not seen a miracle yet in your life, I challenge you to ask God about this, study how He healed in His own ministry while on earth, and begin to ask for miracles, because this passage certainly indicates that His power is alive and well in all ages, in all times.

Pray for miracles as a demonstration of God's power.
Memorization Recommended.

This is how one should regard us,
as servants of Christ
and stewards of the mysteries of God.

- 1 Corinthians 4:1

It is a privilege to be a servant of Christ. We should all revel in the fact that He has made us worthy to be His servants. Look at the Commission He has given us, to be stewards of the mysteries of God. First, we need to know the mysteries of God. In the Gospel of Luke chapter 24, after Jesus' resurrection when he appeared to the Apostles on the road to Emmaus, He explained to them all of the references from the Old Testament that pointed to Him. And their response was "did not our hearts burn within us as He talked to us on the road." The mysteries of God were revealed to them at that time in a new and interior way. The mysteries of God are revealed to us as we spend time with Him, and as we reverence and cherish His holy Word in Sacred Scripture. He promised to remind us of everything that He taught us. And this requires time, we give our time to many things, social media, work, marriage, kids, sporting events and many other things. Do we give time to God, Father, Son and Holy Spirit? Do we give God leftover time that we squeeze in at the end of the day, or do we give Him our prime time? If you want to know the mysteries of God and be stewards of them, you need to give God your prime time. To be a steward, means that we share these mysteries with the world. And the world begins in your own home, in your own neighborhood. Thank you God for making me worthy to be a steward of your mysteries!

Memorization Recommended.

That I may speak a word to the weary,

a word that will rouse them.

- Isaiah 50:4a

Oh my, the weary are all around us. Oftentimes I am
weary, you may be a weary one. How beautiful it is when
God blesses us with a word to rouse one of our brothers
or sisters. A word to rouse the weary may take the form
of a prophetic word, a word of knowledge, or a word
of encouragement that is given to you by God to bless
someone you meet today. Pray that God will give you a
word to rouse the weary today, and that you will have the
courage to speak that word of encouragement into the
life of another today.

Memorization Recommended.

Behold,

I make my words in your mouth a fire.

- Jeremiah 5:14

This is God speaking to the prophet Jeremiah. Notice who makes the words of a prophet effective. It is God Himself, and not the prophet. Is your heart open to being a prophet in today's world? We need prophets today, God is seeking out those who are willing to speak His word. Will that be you? What does fire mean here? It means that the words of the prophet spoken into the life of another sparks a fire in that person's heart. A fire to seek God, a fire to know Him better, a fire that sets their whole life ablaze for love of God.

Memorization Recommended.

*Praised be the God
and Father of our Lord Jesus Christ,
who has bestowed on us in Christ
every spiritual blessing in the heavens.*

- Ephesians 1:3

It is good to be reminded what our life with Christ is supposed to mean. Sometimes we grow a little bit too comfortable with the God of the universe. Here He tells us that in Christ He has poured into us, upon us, for us, for the world, EVERY spiritual blessing in the heavens. My goodness, how many spiritual blessings are there in the heavens? My expectation was and is so much lower. I'm happy if Christ blesses me with one spiritual blessing. It seems He wants more for you and for me. Sometimes we read this in a very selfish fashion and think that these spiritual blessings are for us, and for our own holiness. This is not the case. These spiritual blessings are to equip us to share the Good News and to convert the world. These are spiritual blessings in which we are a vessel and God acts through us. It's as if you are a violin, and the Holy Spirit, who happens to be a virtuoso, picks you up and plays the most beautiful music you have ever heard, and this music goes out into the world for all to hear, love, and believe.

Beseech God to pour out spiritual blessings into your life to equip you for your mission field.

Memorization Recommended.

To be near God is my happiness.

I have made the Lord God my refuge.

I will tell all of his works.

- Psalm 73:28

Equipped with the knowledge of the mysteries of God and every spiritual blessing in heavens, it is now time to go out and share with the world all the works of God!

Choose one of the works of God from your own life and share it with a friend today.

Memorization Recommended.

Behold my servant whom I have chosen,

my beloved in whom I delight,

I shall place my spirit upon him

and he will proclaim justice to the gentiles.

- Matthew 12:18

This passage in Matthew's gospel is a quote from Isaiah chapter 42 It is quoted here after Jesus performed many healings, in fact Matthew chapter 12, verse 15 indicates "he healed them all." The clear indication here is that Jesus is the servant whom God has chosen, Jesus is the beloved in whom God delights in, and that God's own Spirit is in Jesus as He heals and as He proclaims justice to unbelievers. Here in Matthew's gospel, justice takes the form of restoring injured and ill bodies to full health. As the gospels progress, Jesus teaches, equips, and gives authority to not only the 12 apostles, but the disciples and many of His followers. They then go out and do what He did. We are called by our Baptism to do the same. As you go, know that you are the servant God has chosen, you are the one God delights in, you are the one in whom God has placed His Spirit in order to proclaim the Kingdom in your corner of the world.

Spend some time letting God delight in you.

Memorization Recommended.

Just as from heaven
the rain and snow come down
and do not return there
until they have watered the earth,
making it fertile and fruitful,
giving seed to the sower,
and bread to the one who eats.
So shall my word be
that goes forth from my mouth.
It shall not return to me void,
but shall do my will,
achieving the end for which I sent it.

- Isaiah 55:10-11

Look at all that the rain does: waters, makes fertile, makes fruitful, gives seed, gives bread. So too the Word of God: It quenches thirst, pours out the fruit of the Spirit, gives seed that grows into a large plant of faith, and gives nourishment. The words of God are on mission, they have a specific purpose, we are privileged to be the mouthpiece of God in the world. He will soften hearts, He will pour out His love, He will convict of sin, He will pour out mercy. We must simply speak His word. We must be faithful in sowing seeds as the Spirit directs, and in sharing God's word whenever possible.

Share one of your favorite Scripture passages with someone today, be sure to share with them why it is one of your favorites!

I have yet many things to say to you,

but you cannot bear them now.

When the Spirit of Truth comes,

he will guide you into all truth.

- John 16:12

This passage speaks so clearly to the fact that growth in the spiritual life and knowledge of God is real. We begin as small children in faith, and must grow to maturity. God himself longs to share things with us for which we are not yet ready. Woe to us if we do not attend to getting ready. We must also prepare our hearts for the Spirit of truth. We will learn to live with the Spirit of truth, and know that He will empower us at different times in our life with greater and greater outpourings. This is normative Christian life. This is Biblical life. And it's the most adventurous and exciting life we will ever know this side of heaven.

Memorization Recommended

Prepare your heart to receive more of the Spirit of Truth.

All that I have heard from my Father
I have made known to you.

- John 15:15

In the Gospels Jesus is in continual communion and conversation with His Father. He is obsessed with doing the Father's will. And here He tells us clearly that we are in His inner circle. He holds nothing back. Ask Jesus today to share something with you from the Father.

Memorize and expect mysteries of God to be poured into your heart.

Remember the word that I said to you,

a servant is not greater than his master.

If they persecuted me,

they will persecute you.

- John 15:20

As we go on mission in the world, to spread the Good News, to assist in bringing about the Kingdom, we will experience persecution. Just expect it. Jesus did say "pick up your cross and follow me." Crosses are generally not light and fluffy, rather they are rough and heavy. When those persecutions come, don't forget to enact Colossians 1:24, "I rejoice in my sufferings."

Memorization Recommended

11

INDWELLING

To dwell with someone is to live with them in the deepest part of your being. Spouses do this sometimes, in good marriages. God invites us to dwell with Him, and He desires to dwell with us. That is why He sent His Son. This indwelling is a great mystery, one to be contemplated and enjoyed through an entire lifetime. Indwelling will be complete only in heaven. However, this does not mean that we cannot enjoy it now and grow in it!

Come Lord Jesus!

Thank the Lord,
praise the King of the ages
so that his tent may be rebuilt
in you with joy.

- Tobit 13:10

We are encouraged yet again to thank and praise the Lord. He must remind us often, because we often forget. Praise and Thanksgiving are a great way to begin any conversation with the Lord. What does it mean that "his tent will be rebuilt in me with joy?" In the Old Testament, oftentimes a tent was their dwelling, it was their home. We also know the tent of meeting when the Israelites wandered in the desert. We also have the tent where the Ark of the Covenant was kept and reverenced. In this passage, God is indicating that He plans to build His tent in your heart. It needs to be rebuilt because of the ravages and damages of sin. As He works to heal the wounds of sin, our sin and other people's sin upon us, He simultaneously builds His tent, His home in our hearts. This home, this tent, that is being built in our heart, is a place of great joy.

Spend some time in the meeting tent of your heart, enter into the joy which was placed there by the King of the Ages.

Memorization Recommended.

Morning after morning
he opens my ears to hear.

- Isaiah 50:4b

This is a promise. Do we give God a little bit of time in the morning before we begin our day in earnest? Do we wait on Him, for Him to open our ears so that we can hear what it is He wants our day to be about? A practice such as this is not to be taken lightly. It will change your life. Your life will never be the same if you begin your day receiving marching orders from the King!

Tomorrow morning let the Lord open your ears to hear and see what He has to say!

He who is united to the Lord

becomes one spirit with him.

- 1 Corinthians 6:17

Another lovely promise. Our job is to be united to the Lord. His job is to make us one spirit with Him. Being united to the Lord means keeping your eyes fixed on Jesus. It means admitting when you have made a mistake, it means repenting of that mistake. It means striving after virtue, it means being disciplined in penance. It means putting on the mind of Christ, it means knowing scripture. These are all things that we can continue to strive for. And as you do, be watchful for the Lord making you one spirit with Him. He has promised and He will do it, says the Lord!

As you strive to be united to the Lord,
lean into His Spirit.

Do you not know that your body

is a temple of the Holy Spirit within you,

which you have from God?

You are not your own,

you were bought with a price.

So glorify God in your body.

- 1 Corinthians 6:19-20

The truth of this passage is difficult to receive fully. God is saying that our body is a temple. He is saying that the Holy Spirit dwells within us. He is elevating our body to that of Jesus' body. Jesus is the fullness of God and took on human nature. In Jesus, God literally dwelt in the body of a man. Because of our new relationship with God through Baptism, the Holy Spirit now dwells in our body and our body is a temple in which the Holy Spirit lives. It is true that as a Christian we are not our own, we belong to God now. Let us rejoice in belonging to God and let's give God glory in the temple of our body.

Using your body, which is a temple,
raise your arms and clap your hands in praise of God!

May Christ dwell in your hearts

through faith.

\- Ephesians 3:17

It's getting a little crowded in my heart. First the Holy Spirit is there, now Christ is elbowing His way in. My heart must be quite a bit larger than I imagine it to be. Lord, increase my faith! Passages such as these should give us tremendous comfort. When we are having a difficult day, when a friend comes to us with a terrible hurt, we can be assured that God is with us, and near at hand. Proclaim this passage to yourself often.

Memorization Recommended.

Grant us,

in accord with the riches of your glory,

to be strengthened

with power through your Spirit

in the inner self.

- Ephesians 3:15-16

It is more than nice that God desires to strengthen my inner self. But look at the measuring stick for the quantity of strength that will be deposited into me. The measuring stick is "in accord with the riches of His glory." I think Gods' glory has no bounds. He is infinite after all. Also note that God will strengthen us with power. This means His power will be poured out in us, and available to us as we go about sharing the Good News. This also means that growth in the Lord must continue. We have not reached the end of God strengthening us until we reach heaven.

Memorize, believe, and receive!

As a branch cannot bear fruit by itself,

unless it abides in the vine,

neither can you, unless you abide in me.

I am the vine, you are the branches.

He who abides in me and I in him,

he it is that bears much fruit,

for apart from me you can do nothing.

- John 15:4-5

Stay with the vine of Jesus. The sap of the vine, the blood of Jesus, flows in the branches, flows into us. Bear fruit as best you can, so that the vine dresser, the Father, does not prune you off the vine. All we need to do is abide in Jesus, we are not perfect, but He will make us perfect. He lets us take credit for the fruit, but the fruit is truly His. Take heed of the warning that, apart from Jesus we can do nothing, that means absolutely, categorically, nothing. Never take your eyes off Jesus, cling to Him at all times and He will raise you up.

Spend a day imagining yourself as a branch on the vine of Jesus.

In his hand is the soul of every living thing,
and the life breath of all mankind.

- Job 12:10

What a beautiful image: we are in the hand of God. Our very life-breath is held by God in His hand. His nearness is almost frightening. How often during the day do I casually go about my life thinking it is truly my life and not His. The prologue to John's gospel speaks well of how God "holds all things in existence." It would be good for us to bring this to mind several times throughout the day.

Memorization Recommended.

Whoever loves me and keeps my word,

my father will love him,

and we will come to him

and make our dwelling with him.

- John 14:23

When God lavishes His gifts upon us it is easy to love Him. When we experience desolation, and we do not feel God's love and closeness, it is harder to spontaneously love Him. It is important to remember that the continual experience of God and His love will only be ours in heaven. In this life there will be an oscillation between consolation, the experience of God's love, and desolation, the experience of God having abandoned us. This is normal when we are not yet in heaven. Thus we must persevere in loving Him whether we feel Him close or not. This passage also encourages us to keep His word, that means to follow the commandments of the Lord. God's commands lead us and guide us to a happy life. When we do these things, love Him and keep His word, Jesus tells us here that He and the Father will come and make their home with us. Prepare your hearts, people of God, because the Lion of Judah desires to dwell with you!

Memorize, believe, and receive!

There is one thing I ask of the Lord,

for this I long,

to live in the House of the Lord

all the days of my life,

to savor the sweetness of the Lord,

to behold His temple.

- Psalm 27:4

Though we are not in heaven yet, the Lord loves to give us a glimmer, and a taste of things to come. This life is an experience of now, and not yet. As scripture says, "one day within His courts is better than 1000 elsewhere." He will give us these tastes, this sweetness, as we serve Him and love Him unreservedly. These things will be ours as He encourages us on our earthly pilgrimage. Thank you Jesus!

Memorization Recommended.

12

CONCLUSION

We have reached the end of our journey together. I hope it has been a fruitful journey for you. These pages contain some of my most favorite passages that have deepened my relationship with the Lord over the years. For me, I can return to them and always receive more from the Lord. I hope this will be true for you as well. I encourage you to be committed to the Word of God. Though there are different seasons in our life, the Word should always accompany us. Do not be afraid of the ups and downs in your relationship with the Lord, this is natural in this earthly life. We will not have continual happiness and joy until heaven. Thank you for taking this journey with me, keep an eye out for new books. I will be publishing select passages with meditations from individual books in the Bible, and books on individual topics with passages from throughout scripture. May God bless you beyond your imaginings!